The Rotterdam Bar an

With grateful thanks to Chris Pinnock and Lee Barnes.

If you would like to suggest a bar for inclusion or provide updated information regarding an entry, please email feedback@nssales.co.uk

Welcome to Rotterdam

Rotterdam is a bustling Dutch city, overseeing the largest shipping port in Europe. During your trip you'll find a fascinating mix of the old with the new, with historic buildings, stunning modern architecture, impressive museums and a lively night life. Rotterdam is easily reached by plane to Rotterdam The Hague Airport, which is a 20 minute bus ride away. There are plenty of high speed links by train to Rotterdam Central Station, with Amsterdam and Antwerp only about 30 minutes away and even Brussels just over 1 hours journey. By car Rotterdam is conveniently connected to numerous motorways including the A4, A13, A15, A16 and A20. There is also a regular ferry service between Harwich in the UK to the Hook of Holland, which is then about 30 minutes away from central Rotterdam.

Being a strategic harbour during the Second World War much of the city centre was destroyed by heavy German bombing as they sought to quickly occupy the Netherlands. After the war the determined population employed architects to restore the city's former glory and as a result around the centre you'll discover striking modern architecture such as the Cube Houses, De Markthal and Erasmus Bridge. To the west of the centre you'll discover Rotterdam's medieval past in the harbour area known as Delfshaven. This picturesque marina was fortunate to escape the bombing and still contains many historic building. It also marks the location where in 1620 the Pilgrim Father's set sail on their voyage to settle in America.

In this handy guide, we've provided details of what we consider to be the top beer bars/cafes to visit during your stay. You'll also find details of the breweries that are open to visit, the top monuments, attractions and museums that you can visit and the best bottle shops in town. Our aim is to provide the perfect companion for any keen beer tourist during their stay.

Top Rotterdam Bars

1. SS Rotterdam, 3e Katendrechtsehoofd 25. Open Sunday to Thursday 10am to 1am, Friday and Saturday 10am to 2am. Food served. www.ssrotterdam.com
If you are looking for some luxurious relaxation during your visit, why not head to the largest passenger ship ever built in the Netherlands. SS Rotterdam was the former flagship of the Holland America Line and is now permanently moored in Rotterdam. The ship offers a hotel, restaurants, lido and a number of bars which are all open to the public. You'll normally find a beer selection of about 10, along with some interesting local Jenever (Dutch gin). Tours are regularly held if you are interested in finding out more about the history of the ship, see their website for details.

2. Belgisch Biercafé Boudewijn, Nieuwe Binnenweg 53 a-b. Open Sunday to Thursday 12noon to 1am, Friday and Sunday 12noon to 2am. Food available. www.bbcboudewijn.nl
If you enjoy Belgium beer you'll love the Biercafé Boudewijn, as it is basically a brown style Belgium cafe dropped in the heart of Rotterdam. As you would expect the cafe offers around 150 different beers along with a range of traditional Belgium dishes on the food menu. Opened in 2006 and with little to compete from Dutch breweries at the time, it quickly built up a local following with lovers of good beer. Fortunately the Dutch craft beer scene has now developed so there is finally some local competition. **TOP CHOICE**

3. Eetcafe Opa, Witte de Withstraat 49A. Open Monday to Wednesday 4pm to 1am, Thursday and Sunday 12noon to 1am, Friday and Saturday 12noon to 2am. www.eetcafeopa.nl
This modern brasserie offers an excellent range of traditional Dutch dishes, so it's a good place to stop if you are looking for a meal. The beer selection is pretty good as well, with a variety of

Dutch and Belgium beers available. There are plenty of seats out the front on sunny days.

4. Proeflokaal Reijngoud, Schiedamse Vest 148. Open Monday to Thursday 2pm to 1am, Friday to Saturday 12noon to 2am and Sunday 12noon to 1am. Food available. www.proeflokaalreijngoud.nl
Opened in 2012 this is a modern, beer focused, pub that is definitely worth a visit. With 16 beers on draft and more than 100 in bottles there is lots of choice and they regularly have brewery 'take-overs', where they'll offer a full range of drinks from a particular brewery. Food is standard pub grub, but reasonably priced. It can get rather crowded when the football is on TV or if a Beer Pong competition is happening. **TOP CHOICE**

Proeflokaal Reijngoud

5. Melief Bender, Oude Binnenweg 134b. Open Monday 10am to 11pm, Tuesday and Wednesday 10am to Midnight, Thursday 10am to 1am, Saturday and Sunday 10am to 2am. Food available. www.meliefbender.nl

Dating from 1876, this interesting brown bar is actually the oldest cafe in Rotterdam. They stock around 25 beers with 7 on draft, including regular guest beers from the local Brouwerij Noordt. The walls are literally covered with fascinating old photos and antique breweriana.

6. Sijf, Oude Binnenweg 115. Open Sunday and Monday 10am to midnight, Tuesday to Thursday 10am to 1am, Friday and Saturday 10am to 2am. www.sijf.nl

This large and comfortable old fashioned bar offers upper and lower levels inside and a nice outdoor seating area. The impressive beer list contains around 100 to choose from including 8 on draft. They also have a rather good food menu if you are looking for somewhere to eat. **TOP CHOICE**

7. World of Drinks, Grotemarkt 190, Markthal. Monday to Thursday and Saturday 10am to 8pm, Friday 10am to 9pm and Sunday 12noon to 6pm. www.worldofdrinks.com

This off-licence/bar stocks an amazing selection with over 500 different bottles of beer, including a large range from interesting Dutch breweries. You can purchase bottles to take away or enjoy your drink in a seating area on the balcony over-looking the market. A wide range of wines and spirits are also sold.

8. Bokaal, Nieuwemarkt 11. Open Sunday to Thursday 11am to 1am, Friday and Sunday 11am to 2am. Food available. www.bokaalrotterdam.nl

This lively specialist beer bar offers a fantastic selection of beers, decent food and a large patio area for the summer months. The beer menu has over 100 choices available including a section for local beers from Rotterdam. These include the hip new local micro-breweries Kaf & Koren and Drift. **TOP CHOICE**

9. Biergarten Rotterdam, Schiestraat. Outdoor bar open from April; Thursday and Friday 5pm to midnight and from May to September; Tuesday to Saturday 5pm to midnight. Food available. www.biergartenrotterdam.nl

From April until the end of September the square on Schiestraat turns into a lively outdoor bar with DJ's and live bands playing. Stalls offer gourmet burgers and ribs, and the bar offers a range of beers from the Dutch Gulpener brewery on draft. More interesting is the bottle beer selection that usually has around 20 beers from local and international craft breweries. If you like a throbbing crowd it's the place to be.

10. Locus Publicus, Oostzeedijk 364 and Locus International, Oostzeedijk 358B. Open Sunday to Thursday 4pm to 1am, Friday and Sunday 4pm to 2am. Snack food available. (Locus International is closed Sunday and Monday). www.locus-publicus.com

Located in a charmingly characteristic 19th century building Locus Publicus is a stalwart of the local beer scene. The pub serves around 200 different beers, including 15 always on draft, which you'll find listed on various chalk boards around the bar. It has arguably the best selection in Rotterdam, and if that isn't enough in 2014 they opened the Locus International bar two doors down, which has another great range of beers specialising in imported beers from far and wide. **TOP CHOICE**

Locus Publicus

11. Café De Oude Sluis, Havenstraat 7. Open Monday to Thursday from 12noon to 1am, Friday 12noon to 2am, Saturday from 2pm to 2am and Sunday 2pm to 1am. No food served. www.cafedeoudesluis.nl

Located in Delfshaven, the oldest part of the city, this traditional bar dates from 1912 and the interior doesn't look like it has changed much over the years. It's definitely worth checking out if you are in that part of town. The bar offers a pretty decent selection of over 30 beers and there are regular band nights.

12. Tapperij Vanouds 't Kraantje, Schiedamseweg 2A. Open Sunday to Thursday 12noon to 1am, Friday and Saturday 12noon to 2am. No food served. www.biertapperij.nl

Situated in the historic Delfshaven part of the city this large, this old fashioned, locals bar dates from 1912 and stocks a range of around 40 beers. If you're in Delfshaven to visit the Pilgrim brewery then this and Café De Oude Sluis (11) are both worth a visit.

Rotterdam Restaurant Choice

In addition to the bars that serve food on the previous pages, there are a few restaurants we have come across that we feel are worthy of a special mention.

13. Fenix Food Factory, Veerlaan 19d. Open Tuesday to Thursday 10am to 7pm, Friday 10am to 8pm, Saturday 10am to 6pm and Sunday 12noon to 6pm. Closed Monday. www.fenixfoodfactory.nl
Located in a converted old port warehouse this indoor food and drink market will be a hit with any foodies amongst you. The market consists of a number of different stalls offering a wide range of freshly cooked food that can be purchased and eaten in the large seating area. Don't worry, there are stalls selling drinks as well, so you can grab an artisan coffee or pint of beer, depending on what you fancy. See also **Kaapse Brouwers (16)**

14. Ter Marsch & Co, Witte de Withstraat 70. Open Sunday to Thursday 12noon to 1am, Friday and Saturday 12noon to 2am. www.termarschco.nl
It is claimed that his trendy burger restaurant serves the best burgers in the Netherlands, and they certainly are very tasty. Thoughtfully they also offer a range of bottled beers from local micro-breweries so you can also get a decent drink to wash down your meal.

15. Holy Smoke, Tiendplein 1. Open Sunday to Thursday 10.30am to 1am, Friday and Saturday 10.30am to 2am. www.holysmoke.nl
This new restaurant serves prime quality beef, chicken and seafood straight from the grill. They also do a good selection of tasty sandwiches. Better still, the interesting beer menu contains more than 30 choices, mixing old favourites with a range of new craft beers.

Rotterdam Breweries

16. Kaapse Brouwers, Veerlaan 19-D. Open Tuesday to Sunday 12noon to 11pm. Closed Monday. www.kaapsebrouwers.nl
This cool new brewpub is located in the Fenix Food Factory so there is no shortage of good food to accompany your drink. They offer a range of around 30 beers on draft and will often be brewing in the background while you enjoy your drink. You'll usually find a jazz band playing on Friday nights and Sunday afternoons. Beer tasting and food pairing sessions are available to book, see their website for details. An attached bottle shop stocks their full range along with an ample selection from other craft breweries. **TOP CHOICE**

17. Brouwerij Noordt, Zaagmolenkade 46. Open Wednesday to Friday 3pm to 7pm, Saturday and Sunday 2pm to 6pm. Closed Monday and Tuesday. www.brouwerijnoordt.nl
Opened in 2015 this new brewery offers a really good range of craft and specialty beers. Sadly tours aren't available, but from the tap room you can pretty much see all the brewing equipment and fermentation tanks. With up to 20 different beers on draft the tap room is definitely worth a visit. They also stock their range in bottles if you want to take some away. **TOP CHOICE**

Stadsbrouwerij De Pelgrim

18. Stadsbrouwerij De Pelgrim, Aelbrechtskolk 12, Delfshaven. Open Wednesday to Sunday 12noon to midnight. Closed Monday and Tuesday. www.pelgrimbier.nl

In the 1970's when Heineken moved to Zoeterwoude and Oranjeboom to Breda, the city of Rotterdam was left without a brewery. This changed in 1996 with the opening of the Pilgrim Brewery in the historic Delfshaven area of the city. Opened as a pub and restaurant you'll see the brewing equipment as you enter the building. Sadly tours are only available for groups of 8 or more, with details provided on their website. If you stop in for a drink they offer a tasting board, so you can sample all five of their brews. It's also a good place for food, with the menu offering a range of traditional dishes, many of which are prepared with beer from the brewery. **TOP CHOICE**

National Jenever Museum, Schiedam, Lange Haven 74-76, 3111 CH Schiedam. Open Tuesday to Sunday 12noon to 5pm. Closed Monday.   www.jenevermuseum.nl

A short train journey to the west of Rotterdam you'll find the town of Schiedam, the home of the National Jenever (Genever) Museum. Jenever is the forerunner of gin, which was invented by Dutch alchemist Sylvius de Bouve, who infused juniper berries into distilled spirits while attempting to find a cure for stomach disorders. With the Netherlands strong trading history the drink was exported to port cities around the world and gin was born. The Jenever museum is home to the Old Schiedam distillery and there are opportunities to taste the drink (and various fruit flavoured versions) or buy a bottle after a tour.

Beer Festivals

HOP Bierfestival
Held in August each year, this busy beer festival celebrates the latest brews in the lively Dutch craft beer scene. As well as Rotterdam the festival visits Tilburg, Haarlem and Eindhoven. Full details can be found at their website: **www.festival-hop.nl**

Oak Aged Beer Festival
Normally held in March each year at the Pilgrim Brewery, this speciality festival specifically celebrates beers that have been aged in oak barrels. As the barrels have often been used for the storage of spirits, such as bourbon or brandy, this gives the beers very complex and interesting flavours and more often than not knock-out strengths. You'll find full details of this wonderful event at their Facebook page: **www.facebook.com/Oakagedbeerfestival-1435457769926899**

Beer Bottle Shops

7. World of Drinks, Grotemarkt 190, Markthal. Monday to Thursday and Saturday 10am to 8pm, Friday 10am to 9pm and Sunday 12noon to 6pm. www.worldofdrinks.com
This off-licence/bar stocks an amazing selection with over 500 different bottles of beer, including a large range from interesting smaller Dutch breweries. You can purchase bottles to take away or enjoy your drink in a seating area on the balcony over-looking the market. A wide range of wines and spirits are also available.

16. Kaapse Brouwers, Veerlaan 19-D. Open Tuesday to Sunday 12noon to 11pm. Closed Monday. www.kaapsebrouwers.nl
The Kaapse Brouwers micro-brewery that is attached to the Fenix Food Factory have a bottle shop stocking their full range of beers along with a wide selection of several hundred craft beers from the Netherlands and international brewers.

19. Plan B Rotterdam, Gravendijkwal 135. Open Wednesday, Thursday and Saturday 12noon to 7pm, Friday 12noon to 9pm, Sunday 1.30pm to 5.30pm. Closed Monday and Tuesday. www.planbrotterdam.com

Owned by the online shop www.thebeershop-online.com. This impressive bottle shop stocks hundreds of different beers from around the world, including a good selection from Dutch breweries.

Bier&zO

20. Bier&zO, Hoogstraat 54a. Open Tuesday to Friday 11am to 5.30pm and Saturday 10am to 5.30pm. Closed Sunday and Monday. www.bierenzo.nl

Another noteworthy beer shop with hundreds of different bottles available. The range is mainly Belgium and German with a decent selection from Dutch micro breweries.

Top Attractions

A. Kijk-Kubus (Cube Houses), Overblaak 70. Show house is open all week 11am to 5pm. www.kubuswoning.nl

These wonky yellow Cube Houses are one of the most striking pieces of modern architecture in Rotterdam, or indeed anywhere. Designed by architect Piet Blom who wanted to create a village within the city and saw the houses as trees and the whole development area as a wood. The buildings look fantastic from the outside and one of the cubes is open as a museum house, so you can also experience what they are like inside. **TOP CHOICE**

Euromast

B. Euromast, Parkhaven 20. Open every day 10am to 10pm. www.euromast.nl

At 185 metres tall the Euromast is the highest watchtower in the Netherlands and offers a spectacular 360 degree view across Rotterdam and the surrounding area. As well as getting the lift to the top the tower offers a number of other attractions, such as a restaurant at 100 metres, hotel rooms with viewing platform and for thrill-seekers the opportunity to abseil down the outside.

C. Erasmusbrug, Erasmusbrug 1. Open every day.

The Erasmus Bridge is a stunning suspension bridge that spans the River Maas, linking the north and south sections of the city. At 800 metres long and 139 metres high its unusual shape has gained it the nickname The Swan. Fans of the film Who Am I? will recognise the bridge and several other sights in the city as the backdrop to spectacular stunts performed by Jackie Chan.

Erasmus Bridge

D. Laurenskerk, Grotekerkplein 27. Open Tuesday to Saturday 11am to 5pm. Closed Sunday and Monday. www.laurenskerkrotterdam.nl

The Laurenskerk, or Church of St. Lawrence, was built between 1449 and 1525, and after the bombings in the Second World War is central Rotterdam's only surviving late Gothic building. The medieval church still celebrates mass and is also open to the public for tours, concerts and exhibitions. On Wednesday and Saturday from April to October, you can climb the 300 steps to the top of the 63 metre tower for a spectacular view of the city.

E. Boat Trip.

Being a city built around its importance to shipping, it seems a shame not to get onto the water during your stay. There are several companies offering boat trips, the most comprehensive are Spido who depart from the foot of the Erasmus Bridge and offer a number of different tours, full details can be found at their website; www.spido.nl. Other companies offering boat trips include Urban Guides (www.urbanguides.nl) and Splash Tours (www.splashtours.nl). **TOP CHOICE**

F. De Markthal, Ds. Jan Scharpstraat 298. Open daily until 8pm.

This horse-shoe shaped indoor market really is a remarkable sight. If you thought a building comprising housing, restaurants and 100 market stalls wasn't impressive enough, just look up to see the massive artwork 'Horn of Plenty' sprawling across the ceiling like the Sistine Chapel. **TOP CHOICE**

G. Museum Boijmans Van Beuningen, Museumpark 18. Open Tuesday to Sunday 11am to 5pm. Closed Monday. www.boijmans.nl

Opened in 1935 the Museum Boijmans Van Beuningen is one of the oldest museums in the Netherlands. Its contents are built on the legacy from lawyer Frans Jacob Otto Boijmans, who left his art collection to the city of Rotterdam in 1849. Today the museum houses an impressive display, containing many major Dutch and

European masterpieces from the likes of Van Bosch, Degas, Picasso, Van Gogh and Dalí. Highlights include Rembrandt's Titus at his Desk and Breughel's The Tower of Babel. **TOP CHOICE**

Museum Boijmans Van Beuningen is situated on Museumpark, which as the name suggests is a park containing a number of museums and galleries. These include;

H. Chabot Museum, Museumpark 11, is an art-deco style white villa containing a collection of art from Dutch artist Henk Chabot. www.chabotmuseum.nl
I. Natuurhistorisch Museum, Westzeedijk 345, the large Natural History Museum of Rotterdam. www.hetnatuurhistorisch.nl
J. Het Nieuwe Instituut, Museumpark 25, is the Museum of Architecture, Design and Digital Culture. www.hetnieuweinstituut.nl

K. Delfshaven, Aelbrechtskolk 20. Open every day. www.historischdelfshavenrotterdam.nl
This historic harbour dates from 1389, and being slightly out of the city centre was fortunate to escape the bombing in the Second World War that destroyed much of Rotterdam. The picturesque marina is surrounded by many historic buildings dating back to the 17th Century and marks the departure point from which the Pilgrim Fathers sailed for America (via Plymouth). One of these buildings is the Pelgrimsvaderkerk (Pilgrims Fathers Church) which dates from 1417 and contains a number of historical documents and artefacts about this crossing. The church is open alternative Friday and Saturdays from 12noon to 4pm, you can find full details on their website www.oudeofpelgrimvaderskerk.nl. Delfshaven is also home to the Stadsbrouwerij De Pelgrim brewery and a number of pubs listed previously in our bar guide. **TOP CHOICE**

Rotterdam Map Central Area

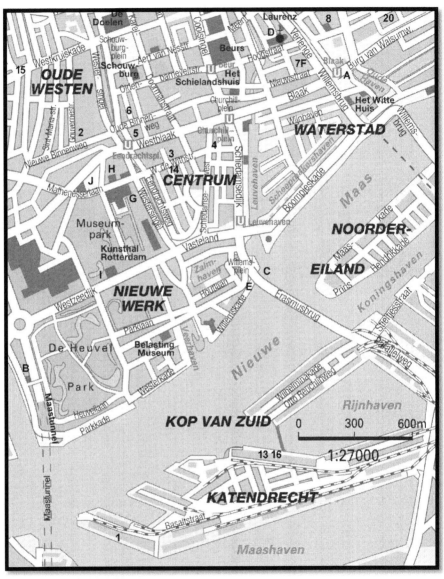

1. SS Rotterdam, 3e Katendrechtsehoofd 25.
2. Belgisch Biercafé Boudewijn, Nieuwe Binnenweg 53 a-b.
3. Eetcafe Opa, Witte de Withstraat 49A.
4. Proeflokaal Reijngoud, Schiedamse Vest 148.
5. Melief Bender, Oude Binnenweg 134b.

6. Sijf, Oude Binnenweg 115.

7. World of Drinks, Grotemarkt 190, Markthal.

8. Bokaal, Nieuwemarkt 11.

13. Fenix Food Factory, Veerlaan 19d.

14. Ter Marsch & Co, Witte de Withstraat 70.

15. Holy Smoke, Tiendplein 1.

16. Kaapse Brouwers, Veerlaan 19-D.

20. Bier&zO, Hoogstraat 54a.

A. Kijk-Kubus (Cube Houses), Overblaak 70.

B. Euromast, Parkhaven 20.

C. Erasmusbrug, Erasmusbrug 1.

D. Laurenskerk, Grotekerkplein 27.

E. Boat Trip.

F. De Markthal, Ds. Jan Scharpstraat 298.

G. Museum Boijmans Van Beuningen, Museumpark 18.

H. Chabot Museum, Museumpark 11.

I. Natuurhistorisch Museum, Westzeedijk 345.

J. Het Nieuwe Instituut, Museumpark 25.

Rotterdam North City Area

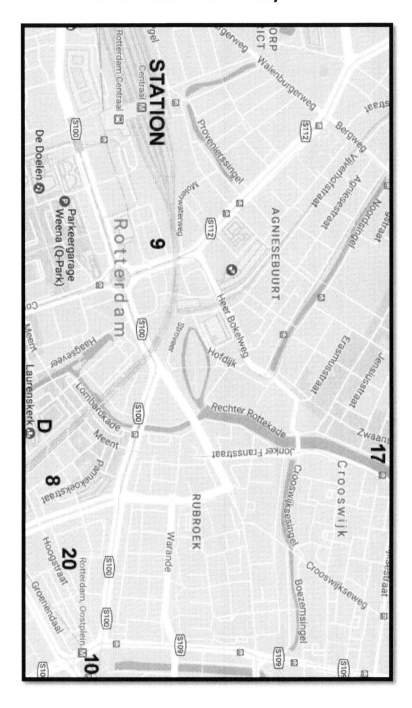

8. Bokaal, Nieuwemarkt 11.

9. Biergarten Rotterdam, Schiestraat.

10. Locus Publicus, Oostzeedijk 364 and Locus International, Oostzeedijk 358B

17. Brouwerij Noordt, Zaagmolenkade 46.

20. Bier&zO, Hoogstraat 54a.

D. Laurenskerk, Grotekerkplein 27.

Rotterdam Delfshaven Area

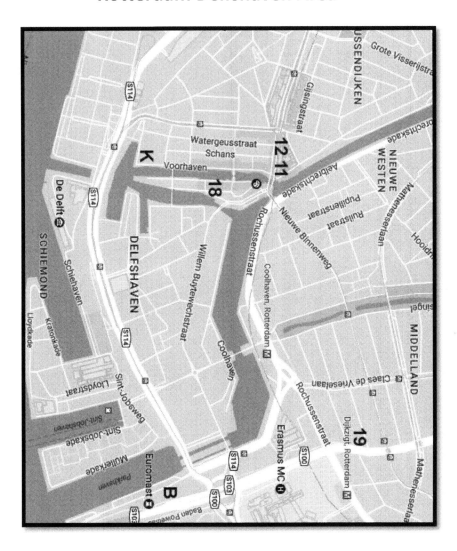

11. Café De Oude Sluis, Havenstraat 7.
12. Tapperij Vanouds 't Kraantje, Schiedamseweg 2A.
18. Stadsbrouwerij De Pelgrim, Aelbrechtskolk 12.
19. Plan B Rotterdam, Gravendijkwal 135.
B. Euromast, Parkhaven 20.
K. Delfshaven, Aelbrechtskolk 20.

.

Printed in Great Britain
by Amazon